This book is dedicated to my son, Nasir Nzegwu. I thank God for you and I am proud, in advance, of the young man you will become.

Daddy loves you, son!

When I wake up in the morning…Daddy tells me to be thankful for another day.

It could be another way.

When I get out of bed…Daddy tells me to be neat, and make my bed.

Life is not always about the things that everyone can see.

When I use the restroom… Daddy tells me to flush the toilet and always clean my hands.

It is easy to spread germs.

When I get in the car…Daddy tells me to buckle my seatbelt.

It is better to be safe than sorry.

When we cross the street... Daddy tells me to look both ways.

It pays to pay attention.

When I go to school…Daddy tells me to listen to my teachers.

When I fall on the soccer field…
Daddy tells me to get back up.

Always do my best and never quit!

When I get frustrated because I can't do something...Daddy tells me to be confident.

I am unique and intelligent.
I can do anything!

When I do not get my way… my Daddy tells me to always listen to my parents.

They know and want the best for me.

When I need anything...
my Daddy is always there and
he always provides.

Actions speak louder than words.

When I ask for something…
Daddy tells me to always say,
"please and thank you."

It is nice and right, to be polite.

My Daddy tells me that no one is better than me, and I am not better than anyone else…

…because we are all equal.

When I ride my bike…
Daddy tells me if I fall down,
pick myself back up.

We may fall down, but what matters most is we get back up and try again.

When I grow up…Daddy tells me I can be anything I want to be.

Put your mind to it, and you can do it!

Every day, my Daddy tells me that he loves me.

…and I tell my Daddy that I love him too!

Now I will show the world what my Daddy told me to do!

The End

About the Author

Chukwuemeka Nonso Nzegwu

C. Nonso Nzegwu is an optimistic, energetic and humbled proud father to his son. His vision for his child and children everywhere is simple: "I don't want you to be like me…I want you to be better than me!" He truly believes that there is always room for improvement. He knows that eventually the mortgage must get paid, but he always remembers that passion is priceless, and you can't buy that!

www.ingramcontent.com/pod-product-compliance
Lightning Source LLC
Chambersburg PA
CBHW041745040426
42444CB00001B/41